NINTH AND JOANIE

Brett C Leonard

I0139938

BROADWAY PLAY PUBLISHING INC
224 E 62nd St, NY, NY 10065
www.broadwayplaypub.com
info@broadwayplaypub.com

NINTH AND JOANIE
© Copyright 2012 by Brett C Leonard

First printing: August 2012
I S B N: 978-0-88145-538-0

Book design: Marie Donovan
Page make-up: Adobe Indesign
Typeface: Palatino
Printed and bound in the U S A

NINTH AND JOANIE was first produced by Labyrinth Theater Company (Artistic Directors, Stephen Adly Guirgis, Mimi O'Donnell & Yul Vázquez; Managing Director, Danny Feldman) in New York. The first performance was on 5 April 2012 witha the following cast and creative contributors were:

ISABELLA.. Rosal Colón
ROCCO .... Kevin Corrigan
MICHAEL .... Dominic Fumusa
CHARLIE .... Bob Glaudini
CARLITO..Samuel Mercedes

Director..Mark Wing-Davey
Scenic design.. David Meyer
Costume design...Mimi O'Donnell
Lighting design .... Bradley King
Sound design...David Bullard
Stage manager..Rhonda Picou
Production manager .... Rosie Cruz
Technical director..Paul Bradley
Special effects ....Jeremy Chernick
Associate director..Paul Bradley
Press representative ....O & M Co

CHARACTERS & SETTING

CHARLIE, *60-70, Italian-American*
ROCCO, *his son, Italian-American*
MICHAEL, ROCCO's *younger brother, Italian-American*
ISABELLA, *mide-20s-30, Puerto Rican from Pittsburgh*
CARLITO, ISABELLA's *and* MICHAEL's *son*

South Philadelphia. 9th Street. 1986.

for those who understand but wish they didn't

ACT ONE

(South Philadelphia. Ninth Street)

(April 1986)

(Martin Sexton's There Go I *is heard, from the beginning.)*

(A well-worn easy-chair. A record turntable. A couch with plastic covering. A coffee table, a couple wooden chairs, end tables, lamps. Framed photo of a 7-year-old girl at her Holy Communion. Above the photo is a wooden crucifix. On another wall is a replica of Renoir's "Mme. Charpentier and Her Children".)

(Leading up the stairs toward unseen overhead floors are a few black and white family photos from the 20s, 30s and 40s.)

(There is a dining room adjacent to the family room. Beyond the wood dining table is a swinging door leading to the kitchen.)

(Newspapers and Daily Racing Forms *in piles on the floor and coffee table. A few dirty glasses, coffee cups and an ashtray with cigar butts.)*

(As the song continues, CHARLIE, *60's/70's, enters the home. Italian-American. He wears a black fedora, black suit, black tie, white shirt, black shoes. He puts his hat on a hook by the front door. He takes off his overcoat and suit coat and drops them on the couch. He takes off his tie and drops it on the couch. He takes off his shoes, leaves his black socks on.*

He takes off his shirt. He wears a long-john thermal shirt underneath—he keeps it on.)

(He takes off his pants and puts them on the couch. He wears thermal long-johns underneath—he keeps them on.)

(He moves to the easy chair. He puts on a pair of brown slippers. He sits. He stares straight ahead. He lifts an unlit cigar off the small table beside him. He bites the end. He spits the tobacco from his mouth, onto the floor. He grabs a pair of blue-tinted swimmer's goggles off the side table. He puts them over his eyes. He lights his cigar. He smokes and stares straight ahead.)

(The music continues.)

(ROCCO enters. Italian-American. He wears a black suit, black tie, white shirt, black shoes. His face is bruised, scabbed and swollen. He puts a set of keys on a small table by the front door. He hangs his coat on a hook.)

(CHARLIE doesn't acknowledge ROCCO as ROCCO walks past him and enters the kitchen. But ROCCO does glance at CHARLIE.)

(CHARLIE smokes. The music plays.)

(ROCCO enters. He has a bottle of Orange Crush with a straw in one hand and a glass of scotch in the other. He puts the scotch on the small table next to CHARLIE.)

(The song no longer plays. Silence)

(ROCCO makes room for himself on the couch. He sits. He drinks soda through the straw.)

(CHARLIE sips the scotch and smokes the cigar.)

(ROCCO rises and looks out the window onto the South Philadelphia street.)

(Pause)

(ROCCO *takes off his shoes, leaves on his black socks. Takes off his tie. Takes off and folds his shirt. He wears a tank-top. His body is bruised, scratched, cut.*)

(ROCCO *looks out the window.*)

(*Pause*)

ROCCO: It's dead out. (*Beat*) There's nobody nowhere.

(ROCCO *stops looking out the window. He looks at* CHARLIE, *who doesn't look at him.*)

ROCCO: Can I open the window? (*Beat*) Huh? (*Pause*) Can I open the window? (*Beat*) It's hot in here.

CHARLIE: It's cold out there.

(ROCCO *finishes his soda, then takes off and folds his pants. He wears boxer shorts. His legs are badly bruised. He looks out the window once again.*)

(*Pause*)

ROCCO: It's not cold.

CHARLIE: You wanna go outside, go outside. (*Beat*) Go outside.

ROCCO: I don't wanna go outside.

CHARLIE: Go outside.

ROCCO: (*Beat*) I wanna stay inside.

(ROCCO *looks out the window.* CHARLIE *smokes.*)

(ROCCO *takes his clothes and shoes, as well as* CHARLIE's, *into his hands. He exits up the stairs.*)

(*Silence as* CHARLIE *smokes and sips his drink.*)

(ROCCO *enters from upstairs. He wears his tank top and boxer shorts. He carries a Ouija board box. He puts the box on the coffee table in front of the couch. He turns and looks at* CHARLIE, *waiting for him to say something.*)

(CHARLIE *says nothing. He doesn't even look at* ROCCO. *He simply smokes, drinks, stares straight ahead.*)

(ROCCO *takes his empty Orange Crush bottle into the kitchen. He returns with another Orange Crush, sipping on the straw.*)

(*He sits on the couch. He opens his Ouija board box. He looks at* CHARLIE. *He opens the board and takes out the planchette. He looks at* CHARLIE. *He puts his fingers on the planchette. He looks at* CHARLIE. *He closes his eyes. The planchette begins to move.*)

(CHARLIE *looks at him. Then looks away.*)

(ROCCO *takes his hand off the planchette and wipes his brow. He looks at* CHARLIE. *He closes his eyes again, fingers once again on the planchette.*)

(*He stops. Wipes his brow. Looks at* CHARLIE, *who pays him no mind.*)

ROCCO: Can I turn on the fan? (*Beat*) Huh? (*Beat*) Pop? Can I turn on the fan? (*He stands and moves to a fan plugged into a wall. He turns it on.*) Is that okay? The level? (*Beat*) It's okay?

(*No response from* CHARLIE)

(ROCCO *goes to the couch. Sits. He puts his hands on the planchette and closes his eyes. He talks to* CHARLIE, *who seems to ignore him.*)

ROCCO: (*Eyes remain closed*) I'm 'unna bring her come visit, Pop. (*Beat*) Ya heard? (*Beat*) I'm 'unna call her back visit. (*Beat*) You heard? (*Pause*) I seen Joanie like that too. (*Beat*) I seen'r like that lotta times. (*Beat*) I seen'r right there where you sittin'. Eatin' ice cream in your chair. (*Beat*) I know what I seen.

CHARLIE: That isn't very Christian. You and your Wee-gee, Rock. (*Beat*) It isn't very *Catholic*. (*He holds out his glass.*)

ROCCO: Another one?

(CHARLIE *says nothing, continues to hold out his glass.*)

(ROCCO *rises, takes the glass from his father's hand and exits into the kitchen.*)

(CHARLIE *smokes and stares straight ahead.*)

(ROCCO *returns with the drink, puts it on the table next to* CHARLIE. ROCCO *returns to his spot on the couch with the Ouija Board.*)

(CHARLIE *sips his drink.*)

ROCCO: It's Ouija. (*No response, beat*) You said "wee-gee". (*No response, beat*) It's Oui-*ja*. Not *gee*. (*No response, beat*) In French "oui" means "yes". And in German "ja" means "yes". "*Oui...Ja*". (*No response, beat*) "Yes-yes". "Oui-ja".

CHARLIE: Am I French?

ROCCO: Huh?

CHARLIE: Am I French?

ROCCO: No.

CHARLIE: Am I German?

ROCCO: No.

CHARLIE: Are you?

ROCCO: I'm Italian.

CHARLIE: So am I. (*He looks away. Drinks, smokes*)

(*Pause*)

(ROCCO *moves to the window.*)

ROCCO: Everyone's inside. (*Beat*) No one in the park neither. I never seen it like this.

CHARLIE: What time is it? (*Beat*) What time is it?

(ROCCO *checks his watch.*)

ROCCO: Almost nine.

CHARLIE: Turn on the T V.

ROCCO: You wanna watch T V?

CHARLIE: That Spic tonight's on the T V. Turn it on.

ROCCO: *(Remembering)* Oh yeah.

(ROCCO turns on the old, wood-encased television. He flips channels. We Hear Geraldo Rivera apologizing to the television audience for finding nothing more than dirt, a few gin bottles and a Stop-Sign.)

(CHARLIE snuffs out his partially-smoked cigar in the ashtray beside him. He takes off the swimmer's goggles and puts them next to the ashtray, as we hear: Geraldo Rivera [on T V] "I promised all the critics that if we didn't find anything I'd sing a song, so, uh...uh... 'Chicago, Chicago, that toddlin' town'... Alright, I'm gone... I'll see ya...")

CHARLIE: Turn it off.

(ROCCO turns off the T V.)

CHARLIE: Look outside in two minutes. There's your respect.

(CHARLIE finishes his scotch. He stands, empty glass in hand and exits toward the kitchen. ROCCO watches him. Then ROCCO looks out the window, checks his watch.)

(CHARLIE enters with a box of pretzels and a fresh scotch.)

CHARLIE: Every moron now in the neighborhood. They wouldn't recognize Al Capone if he knocked on the door. *(He sits.)*

ROCCO: I'd recognize him.

CHARLIE: You wouldn't recognize me.

ROCCO: I'd recognize you. *(Beat)* Pop? *(Beat)* I'd recognize you. *(Beat)* I'd recognize Al Capone too. *(Beat)* I got a book upstairs.

CHARLIE: You got a book.

ROCCO: Upstairs.

CHARLIE: Every Guinea's got a book.

ROCCO: Wha'does that mean?

CHARLIE: Why donchya go read it?

ROCCO: What?

CHARLIE: Go upstairs and read your book. (*He puts the unlit cigar in his mouth. He puts the goggles over his eyes.*)

ROCCO: I don't wanna.

(CHARLIE *lights his cigar.*)

ROCCO: I don't wanna read my book.

CHARLIE: Every Guinea watchin' the Spic on T V. Rocco has a book.

ROCCO: I got a lotta books.

(CHARLIE *smokes, staring straight ahead.*)

(*Pause*)

ROCCO: I got all kinda books. (*He looks outside. He looks to* CHARLIE.) You hungry? (*Beat*) Pop? (*No response. He looks out the window.*) They musta all been watchin' T V. There's a lotta people now.

(CHARLIE *looks at* ROCCO. *Point proven*)

(*Beat*)

ROCCO: Ya want me to make ya some'n to eat?

CHARLIE: I got pretzels.

ROCCO: I'm startin' ta get hungry.

CHARLIE: You're startin' ta get fat.

ROCCO: I ain't fat.

CHARLIE: Ya get fat, ya get black an' blue—same thing.

ROCCO: It's not the same thing.

CHARLIE: Same thing.

ROCCO: I'm hungry. (*He exits to the kitchen.*)

CHARLIE: Rock? (*Beat*) Rocky? (*Beat*) Rocco!

(ROCCO *enters, stands in the doorway between the living room and kitchen.*)

CHARLIE: I wanna hear my music.

(ROCCO *doesn't move.*)

CHARLIE: Put it on, wouldja? (*Beat*) Rock?

ROCCO: Yeah. Sure, Pop. (*He moves for the stereo.*)

CHARLIE: Not too loud.

ROCCO: Yeah.

(ROCCO *leans over the turntable and gently puts the needle on the appropriate groove. Vic Damone's* An Affair to Remember *is heard. He stands and listens, his head down.* CHARLIE *listens. They listen in silence to the entire song.*)

(*When it ends,* ROCCO *lifts the needle off the record.*)

(*Pause*)

ROCCO: Ya wan' me to play it again? (*Beat*) Pop?

CHARLIE: (*Beat*) No.

ROCCO: (*Beat*) Ya wan' me to put a different song?

CHARLIE: ...No.

(CHARLIE *holds out his empty scotch glass.* ROCCO *takes the glass from his father's hand.*)

(ROCCO *exits, into the kitchen.*)

(*Pause*)

ROCCO: (*Loudly from the kitchen*) I'm makin' ham an' cheese, Pop. I ain't that hungry if ya wanna split halfs. We got peppers an' onions. Got the rolls from Sarcone's. I could make it not too much oil, lotta vinegar like ya like, gotta watch calories anyway, I don't mind.

(CHARLIE *snuffs out his cigar. He takes the goggles off his eyes. He takes a pretzel from the box, stands, and slowly*

exits—up the stairs toward the second floor, as ROCCO
continues:)

ROCCO: *(Still in the kitchen)* I ain't said I don't haveta
lose weight, I juss said I ain't fat. Ain't too fat, but I
know, I know I do. It's juss I get things I fight an' get
hold a' take effect sometimes, things I can't explain. I
gotta build up more 'fore I can let 'em out, things ain't
done buildin'. My Ouija tells me I gotta wait, ain't
time. In due time. But you're right, Pop, I know, I'm
tryin', try harder soon too. You'll see. I'm 'unna try
like I know an' do better even after that. Ain't no room
for no sissies. Ain't *time*, right Pop? Time for *men*, not
boys—sissies maybe got *some* place but that place ain't
South Philly, right Pop? Ain't Ninth Street. My Ouija
tells me the same thing. Tells me things like, keep
goin'...don't stop...things gotta improve someday.

*(*MICHAEL *enters through the front door. Italian-American.*
ROCCO's *younger brother. He wears brown slacks, an un-
tucked, button-up shirt and brown shoes. He carries a black
duffel bag.)*

*(He closes the door behind him and puts the duffel bag on the
floor.)*

(He lights CHARLIE's *cigar. He puts on the goggles, moves
for the stereo. All the while,* ROCCO *continues shouting from
the kitchen:)*

ROCCO: I *gotchya*, me an' you Pop, I gotchya—I got
strength 'nuff for the both a' us. I got strength 'nuff
this whole town. This whole *state*! You wan' a orange
soda with your hoagie? I could give ya one a' mine.
I'll watch I don't eat so much calories, you watch you
don't drink so much. Like a wager, only friendly. An'
only if ya wanna. If ya don't wanna, we don't haveta.

*(*MICHAEL *removes the Vic Damone record and puts a
different record on the turntable.)*

ROCCO: I could bring ya another scotch instead. Or a glass a' red wine. Ya want red wine, Pop? Chianti? Pop, ya want wine? Pop? Or another scotch? Or I could give ya one a' my Orange Crushes too.

(MICHAEL *lowers the needle onto the record—Stevie Ray Vaughn's live version of* Mary Had a Little Lamb *[from the Scorsese Collection]).*

ROCCO: Pop, you hear me? Pop? Why're ya lissenin' to that for, that's my record. Pop?

(MICHAEL *turns the volume up louder.)*

ROCCO: POP?!

(MICHAEL *turns the volume louder.)*

ROCCO: WHADDAYA WANNA DRINK? CAN YOU HEAR ME?

(MICHAEL *turns the volume even louder.)*

ROCCO: POP?! POP?!

(MICHAEL *turns the music louder.)*

ROCCO: WHY YA LISSENIN' TA THAT? POP?! *(He emerges in the doorway between the kitchen and living room.)*

(MICHAEL *stands, cigar in mouth, goggles over his eyes, smiles, dances a little.)*

ROCCO: What're ya doin?

(MICHAEL *turns the volume way up—blasting—begins to dance in the middle of the room.)*

(ROCCO *moves to the turntable, lifts the needle off the record...as:)*

ROCCO: WHAT'RE YA DOIN'?!

(MICHAEL *moves back to the turntable, puts the needle back on the record, music blasts, he dances. And sings:)*

MICHAEL: *(Sings)* "Mary had a little lamb, whose face was black as coal, yeah, everywhere that child went, ya know the lamb was sure ta go, yeah."

(ROCCO lifts the needle off the record.)

ROCCO: I think Pops takin' a nap.

MICHAEL: May we be so lucky he never wakes. May we be so lucky to stuff him the trunk of a car. You got a car, Rock?

ROCCO: No.

MICHAEL: Me neither. Maybe we could shove him the trunk of a neighbor's car. Is Aunt Rose still next door?

ROCCO: Aunt Rose died more'n two years ago.

MICHAEL: How bout Uncle Eddie, ya think he'll let us use his car?

ROCCO: Uncle Eddie's dead too.

MICHAEL: Uncle Carlo, he dead?

ROCCO: Found'm Palumbo Park—one ta the back a' the head.

MICHAEL: *(Quoting* CHARLIE*)* "Without codes and consequences, what are we, Rocky? Monkeys throwin' shit in a cage." We are the spawn of a drunk man's sperm. And that sperm whale is upstairs tryin' ta sleep. *(He puts the needle on the record and dances, sings:)* "He followed her to school one day and broke the teacher's rule - what a time that they had that day at school." HIT IT, ROCK!

(ROCCO doesn't move. MICHAEL *dances.)*

MICHAEL: Move it, Rock, yeah—dance baby, move— shake it, Rocky—look out!

(ROCCO turns off the music. MICHAEL *stops dancing, opens his arms and smiles, as if there is no past between them:)*

MICHAEL: Hello Rocky.

ROCCO: *(Turns to face* MICHAEL*)* I think the music mighta woke him.

MICHAEL: Maybe he's dead an' couldn't hear it.

ROCCO: It was loud enuff he'da woke he was dead.

MICHAEL: Yeah?

ROCCO: It was pretty loud, Mike.

MICHAEL: So ya think if we dug up Ma we could play some loud music, wake'r up?

ROCCO: I didn't say nuthin' bout Mom.

MICHAEL: I did. *(He takes off the goggles and moves toward the kitchen.)*

ROCCO: *(As if* MICHAEL*'s headed upstairs)* Where ya goin'?

*(*MICHAEL *ignores him, enters the kitchen.* ROCCO *remains. He removes the Stevie Ray Vaughn record from the turntable.)*

*(*MICHAEL *enters, drinking from a jug of cheap, red wine.)*

MICHAEL: You got fat, Rock.

ROCCO: You got skinny.

*(*MICHAEL *looks at the photo of the young girl.)*

ROCCO: Ya got here late, Mike.

MICHAEL: *(Still looking at the photo)* Trains.

ROCCO: Yeah.

MICHAEL: *(Looking at the photo)* I don't have a car.

ROCCO: Me neither.

MICHAEL: *(Looking at the photo)* Right, that's why we gotta borrow from someone else. *(Looks at* ROCCO*)* How was the service?

ROCCO: I dunno. *(Beat)* Sad. *(Beat)* Real sad. *(Beat)* You weren't there. *(Beat)* I thought I mighta seen ya there, but...

MICHAEL: No.

ROCCO: No.

MICHAEL: I'm here now.

ROCCO: I mean sooner, Mike. Sooner-sooner. A lot sooner.

MICHAEL: C'mere.

ROCCO: Ma never said, but I think she felt the same.

MICHAEL: C'mere. Get over here.

ROCCO: I don't wanna.

MICHAEL: Rocco.

ROCCO: No.

MICHAEL: *(Moving to* ROCCO*)* Give your brother a hug.

*(*MICHAEL *hugs* ROCCO*.* ROCCO *doesn't hug him back. While holding* ROCCO *in his arms:)*

MICHAEL: You're okay.

ROCCO: Yeah.

MICHAEL: Say okay.

ROCCO: Okay.

MICHAEL: Okay. *(He kisses* ROCCO*'s cheek, moves away.)* How long ago he go ta sleep?

ROCCO: I don't know he's even sleepin'.

MICHAEL: That's what you said.

ROCCO: I know.

MICHAEL: But you don't know.

ROCCO: I know he ain't here.

MICHAEL: Ain't here *here*, in the house here, or ain't here downstairs?

ROCCO: I didn't hear'm leave.

MICHAEL: You didn't hear me enter.

ROCCO: Wan' me ta go check?

MICHAEL: I'll wait. *(He goes to the window, looks out.)* How many a' them kids ya think'll ever see the Statue of Liberty?

ROCCO: I ain't never seen the Statue of Liberty.

MICHAEL: You ain't never seen the Liberty Bell.

ROCCO: I have to. I seen the Liberty Bell, Mike. I seen the Liberty Bell a few times. I seen the Liberty Bell four times.

(MICHAEL continues looking out the window.)

(Pause)

ROCCO: It was dead earlier. No one. *(Beat)* Nuthin'. *(Beat)* Geraldo opened Capone's vault. On the T V— Geraldo Rivera—he opened Al Capone's vault. There was no one on the street. They only found a coupla bottles. And a Stop sign. I don't think it was his vault. I got a book about him. *(Beat)* I think they got the wrong vault.

(MICHAEL briefly looks overhead.)

ROCCO: Dija hear him? Wan' me ta go check?

MICHAEL: *(Looks to ROCCO)* No.

ROCCO: Ya sure?

(MICHAEL drinks.)

ROCCO: I think he'll be happy ta see ya. You were always his favorite. I mean—other'n Joanie. It was Joanie most, an' then you. Moms was the opposite—it was you first, then Joanie. *(Beat)* He'll be glad ta see ya, Mike. Ya sure ya don't want me ta go check?

MICHAEL: Let'm sleep.

(MICHAEL goes to the window again. He takes turns looking out the window, then at his brother, briefly skimming a Racing Form, *drinking... As* ROCCO *continues...)*

ROCCO: There was no one when we got home - no one. I thought... I dunno. I thought maybe... maybe everyone was inside cuz a' *her*, ya know? Juss... everyone 'cidin' not ta go out, not ta have fun on account a' her. And what maybe we was goin' through. Outta respect. We didn't say nuthin' durin' the ride home, 'cept Pop mutterin' keep eyes on the meter, make sure the nigger cabbie don't take us for a run. Pops went in the house before me, when we got back, but... I couldn't. I went down Ninth, there was no one. No one on a stoop, no one in the park. I pictured everyone musta loved Ma or feared Pop so much they was inside prayin' or some'n. Like insteada throwin' a parade or comin' ta the church or the cemetery. Outta respect. I walked the other way, ta Lombard. They was out up there, the Blacks, on the other side. But still nuthin' this side, our side. I go there sometimes, y'know? Ta the corner. I think about Joanie. I go sometimes when I don't even mean ta, I just find I'm standin' there—right there on that corner. An' everytime, tonight was the same, seein' as there's no marker or nuthin', I leave some kinda mark a' my own. Some'n ta remember her by. No one else has ta know what it is, but I know. An' sometimes other people gotta see and take a moment I think too, even if justa wonder why it's there—and her name—I always write her name. *(Beat)* I left Ma's funeral card tonight. I put it on the curb, under a rock, the same spot they found them two little pieces a' Joanie's skull. There's no way for anyone ta know that. That they're steppin' where her skull was. I don't blame 'em, ya can't blame people for what they don't know, but I try ta make'm know. Seein' as there's no marker. Tonight I wrote a note an' left it with Ma's funeral card. A note said, "Mom and Joanie, you are together again. With love from your son and brother. Rocco." *(Beat—damn!)* I shoulda put your name on it too.

MICHAEL: It's okay—

ROCCO: —We could go back if ya want and add your name—

MICHAEL: —Don't worry about it—

ROCCO: —We could go a little later too—

MICHAEL: —It's alright—

ROCCO: —Or when Pop wakes. Or I could go wake'm now and—

(MICHAEL's temper explodes:)

MICHAEL: —I WANT MY NAME I'LL PUT MY OWN FUCKIN' NAME! WHY THE FUCK WOULD I NEED YOU?! YOUR IDEAS ARE FOR SHIT, ROCCO! FOR GODDAMN SHIT! *(He drinks from the jug of wine.)*

(Long pause)

ROCCO: I understand...Mike. Michael. *(Beat)* I understand.

(ROCCO takes the Ouija board to the dining room table. He sits. He stares down at the board. He doesn't touch the planchette. He continues to stare at the board. Pause)

ROCCO: Are ya hungry? *(Beat)* Mmph? *(Beat)* I was makin' a hoagie when ya came. *(Beat)* I could run ta Isgro for cannoli. I know how much ya like Isgro.

MICHAEL: It's late, Rock, they're closed.

ROCCO: I know a guy works there. He's got keys.

MICHAEL: It's okay.

ROCCO: We got Tastykake in the fridge.

MICHAEL: It's okay...Rocky. *(Beat)* Thank you.

ROCCO: Okay. Maybe in the morning then.

MICHAEL: Maybe. *(He moves for his duffel bag, picks it up, moves to the couch, as:)*

ROCCO: *(Beat)* I'm 'unna save ya half a hoagie anyways, case ya change your mind. *(Beat)* I got the rolls from Sarcone's. *(He looks down at his Ouija board. He closes his eyes, he puts his hands over the planchette. He hesitates, looks at his brother.)* How long ya gonna stay for?

MICHAEL: I'm not.

ROCCO: Oh. I thought... Cuz your bag.

(MICHAEL puts the duffel bag on his lap.)

MICHAEL: Coat an' tie. An' a white shirt. In case I made the service. *(Beat)* An' black shoes.

ROCCO: I got clothes if ya want.

MICHAEL: Thank you.

ROCCO: I got clothes for days. You could stay in your old room. I got a lotta clothes.

(CHARLIE appears, walking slowly down the stairs. ROCCO looks, then looks at MICHAEL, who stands, duffel bag against his chest. ROCCO looks back at CHARLIE.)

(CHARLIE ignores them and moves toward the kitchen.)

ROCCO: Mikey's home, Pop.

(No response)

ROCCO: Mikey's home.

(CHARLIE enters the kitchen.)

(ROCCO looks at MICHAEL. MICHAEL stares at the kitchen's swinging door, duffel bag still at his chest.)

(ROCCO closes his eyes, puts his hands on the planchette. His hands begin to move across the Ouija Board.)

(CHARLIE enters from the kitchen, drink in hand. He sits in his easy chair, puts on his goggles, lights his cigar.)

(ROCCO speaks with his eyes closed, his hands moving slowly about the Ouija Board.)

ROCCO: *(Eyes closed)* I seen Joanie last week. I seen'r in Pops' chair, sittin' in it...eatin' ice cream. I seen'r the bottom a' the stairs too. In her communion dress. She looked pretty. I seen'r in the cellar, by Ma's sewin' machine. She wasn't sewin', she was watchin' Ma sew. The two of us tagether. We was watchin' Ma sew.

(MICHAEL stares at his father. CHARLIE continues to drink, smoke and ignore. ROCCO opens his eyes, he looks at the Ouija board. He looks at CHARLIE.)

ROCCO: Mike's home, Pop. *(Beat)* Pop? *(Beat)* Mikey came back home.

CHARLIE: This ain't his home.

ROCCO: He came for the service. He was late cuz a' problems with the trains. He don't have a car. I told'm that's okay. I told'm I don't have one neither.

CHARLIE: You have a book...Rocco. Ain't that right? A book and a Ouija board. *(Beat)* Where ya been, Michael?

MICHAEL: *(Beat)* Pittsburgh. *(Beat)* Mostly.

(CHARLIE has no response, no reaction.)

MICHAEL: I been ta New York too.

ROCCO: He seen the Statue a' Liberty.

CHARLIE: *(To MICHAEL)* You got skinny.

MICHAEL: A little.

CHARLIE: I'm the same to the pound. That's important. Ta take care a' yourself. *(Beat)* Get me another drink, Rock. See if your brother wants one.

(ROCCO doesn't move. CHARLIE holds out his glass.)

CHARLIE: Rocky?

(ROCCO doesn't answer.)

CHARLIE: Rocco? Get me a drink and whatever your brother wants too.

MICHAEL: *(Re: CHARLIE's drink)* Same.

(CHARLIE continues to hold out his empty glass. ROCCO takes it and exits into the kitchen.)

(MICHAEL looks at CHARLIE. CHARLIE doesn't look at him.)

(Long pause)

CHARLIE: I been ta Pittsburgh once. *(Beat)* That was enough.

(ROCCO returns with the drinks. He hands one to CHARLIE, one to MICHAEL, who drinks it down straight. ROCCO sits at the dining room table and drinks an Orange Crush through a straw.)

(Pause)

(Then, CHARLIE speaks. Calmly, slowly, not looking at either of his sons until he directly addresses MICHAEL:)

CHARLIE: Your mother loved your sister very much. I never wanted a daughter but I loved her very much too. An angel after the two of you. *(Beat)* I buried my mother. I buried my father. I buried four brothers and two sisters. *(Beat)* Today I buried my wife. *(Beat)* And fifteen years ago I buried your sister. Thirteen years old. It wasn't cancer. It wasn't God. It was a drunk-driver-spic-nigger. Now he's dead too. *(Beat)* There is nothing worse on this earth than burying one of your own. You do in who did in yours. It's what gets done.

I find peace in that. I find *peace*...knowin' that half-breed spic-nigger burns in hell. That's my peace. But it was not your *mother's* peace. Your mother's peace was having good kids. Your mother's peace was being a better mother than her mother. And you *took* that... Michael. You ran off at the mouth, what you did, why you did it...you ripped your mother's peace right outta her heart. *(He snuffs out his cigar. He removes his goggles.)* She never needed to know the *words*. The *facts* that didn't concern her and would only make her upset. Getting those *thoughts*. Getting those little boy *lies* about who mighta asked you, who mighta not, *cryin'*, *confessin'* in her ear, *blaming*—

MICHAEL: —They weren't lies.

CHARLIE: You didn't attend your own mother's funeral.

ROCCO: He got here late, Pop.

CHARLIE: *(To* ROCCO*)* I'm not talking to you. *(Beat)* Do you understand? I am not talking to you.

MICHAEL: They weren't lies.

CHARLIE: You knew exactly what you were doing.

MICHAEL: I never tried to hurt her.

CHARLIE: You succeeded in everything you ever tried.

MICHAEL: I didn't try.

CHARLIE: You were her favorite, Michael.

MICHAEL: I didn't try.

CHARLIE: You got away with everything your whole life.

MICHAEL: Not everything, Pop.

CHARLIE: It's the only decent thing you ever did.

MICHAEL: It's what you wanted.

CHARLIE: I'm gonna lay down.

(CHARLIE *rises, moves for the stairs.*)

MICHAEL: Codes and consequences, honor... You asked Rocco first—

CHARLIE: —Some things don't haveta get asked—

MICHAEL: —I did what you wanted!—

CHARLIE: (*To* MICHAEL: *calm but direct*) —Your mother slit her throat with a steak knife—

ROCCO: —STOP—

MICHAEL: —I did what he couldn't—

CHARLIE: —She took a knife across her own neck—

ROCCO: —STOP!—

MICHAEL: —What needed ta be done—

CHARLIE: —Your sister was *dead*, you killed that Spic-Nigger and nobody needed to know—

ROCCO: —STOP IT!—

CHARLIE: (*Suddenly explodes*) —SHUT THE FUCK UP, ROCKY, SHUT UP! (*Then, calmly to* MICHAEL) Telling your mother what you did, did no good. Telling her I told you to, did no good.

MICHAEL: You did.

CHARLIE: I did or I didn't. You went to jail. She loses two children the same week. She's got a dead daughter, a murdering son, a husband she thinks told you to do it... (*Re:* ROCCO) And this one over here... (*Beat*) The only question is...what took her so long. (*Heads for the stairs, his back to* MICHAEL) It's good ta see ya, Mike. You can spend the night if ya like.

MICHAEL: You told me my whole life. You told me my whole life.

(CHARLIE *continues up the stairs as:*)

MICHAEL: "A boy ain't a man at eighteen, some boys are never men. You will be a man when you act like a man! Your birth certificate means nothing! Take *ACTION*, Michael—*DO* something."

(CHARLIE *disappears up the stairs. From downstairs:*)

MICHAEL: "When *hit* hit back! Be a man, not a little boy! Your birth certificate means shit!" POP?! *(Beat)* POP?! *(Pause. He drinks from the bottle of wine.)*

ROCCO: You alright? *(Beat)* Mikey? *(Beat)* You okay?

MICHAEL: ...Mmph?

ROCCO: Are you alright?

MICHAEL: What else we got to drink?

ROCCO: What?

MICHAEL: Bring me it. *(He finishes the bottle of wine.)*

ROCCO: Bring you what?

MICHAEL: What you have to drink. Bring me all of it.

ROCCO: All of it?

MICHAEL: We're gonna drink all of it.

ROCCO: I don't drink.

MICHAEL: *(Yeah, right)* Since when?

ROCCO: Since I didn't wanna anymore.

MICHAEL: Why not?

ROCCO: I didn't wanna be who I was.

MICHAEL: How bout *now*...Rock... Do you wanna be who you are right now?

ROCCO: Sometimes.

MICHAEL: Right now this second? Do you wanna be who you are *right now*?

ROCCO: I dunno.

MICHAEL: You're still gettin' in fights, right?

ROCCO: Sometimes.

MICHAEL: Every night?

ROCCO: Sometimes.

MICHAEL: Sometimes?

ROCCO: I don't hit back no more.

MICHAEL: Ya gotta hit back.

ROCCO: No I don't!

MICHAEL: Ya gotta do *something*. Fight back or stop fighting. Do something, Rocky, fuckin' do it, do it!—

ROCCO: —*Stop*—

MICHAEL: —Do it!—

ROCCO: —*Leave me alone*—

MICHAEL: —Ya never did *nothing*! *I did something, you did shit!* Do something!—

ROCCO: —Stop!—

MICHAEL: —DO SOMETHING!!—

ROCCO: —NO!—

MICHAEL: —Do it! Do it!—

ROCCO: —NOT YET!—

MICHAEL: —Do it, Rocky, *something*!—

ROCCO: *(Explodes with rage)* —I'M GONNA DO WHAT I WANNA DO, WHAT I WANNA DO IS WHAT I'M *GONNA* DO, DON'T TELL ME WHAT TA DO!—

MICHAEL: —Okay—

ROCCO: —DON'T TELL ME!—

MICHAEL: —Okay—

ROCCO: —I'M 'UNNA GET IN SHAPE MICHAEL! I'M 'UNNA BE ME AGAIN! I'M 'UNNA HIT BACK

AGAIN! I'M 'UNNA PICK THE BIGGEST TWO IN
THE BAR HOW I USETA ONLY THIS TIME I'M
GONNA BE *SOBER!* MY AGE WON'T MATTER CUZ
I'M 'UNNA BE SOBER AN' STRONG AND THE
PAST WON'T MATTER NEITHER! ONLY *SOME*
PAST! THE PAST I *WANNA* MATTER! I'M BUILDIN'
IT UP, MIKE! MY *PAST!* IT'S BUILDIN', AN' I'M
'UNNA DISH IT OUT WHAT'M BUILDIN' AN' I
DON'T NEED YOU TA TELL ME NO DIFFERENT!
YA RUN OFF TA PRISON RUNNIN' OFF THE
MOUTH TA MOMMA, MAKE'R DO NUTTIN' BUT
SIT DOWNSTAIRS AN' *SEW,* COME BACK RUNNIN'
OFF THE MOUTH THE SAME WAY, SHUT UP! LET
'EM HIT ME, MIKE! LET 'EM ALL HIT ME, AN'
HIT ME, AN' HIT ME, AN' HIT!! I'M BUILDIN' IT
UP AN' THEN I'M GONNA TEAR IT DOWN. I'M
GONNA *HURT* PEOPLE, MIKE. I'M 'UNNA MAKE
'EM *BLEED!* BUT I AIN'T DONE AN' WHEN I'M
DONE IS WHEN I'M DONE AN' THAT'S BETWEEN
ME AN' WHOEVER IT'S BETWEEN, NOT YOU! RUN
OFF AT THE MOUTH WITH SOMEONE ELSE CUZ I
DON'T WANNA LISTEN NO MORE AN' MOMMA'S
SOMEWHERE OUTSIDE DEAD! *(He turns and moves
for the kitchen.)*

MICHAEL: Where ya goin'?

ROCCO: I'm gettin' ya somethin' for yer mouth! *(He
exits into the kitchen.)*

*(*MICHAEL *goes to the stereo. He puts on Stevie Ray
Vaughn's live version of* Mary Had a Little Lamb.*)*

(He turns it up a little louder. And louder)

*(*ROCCO *enters, carrying a box of bottles.)*

ROCCO: He's tryin' ta sleep!

MICHAEL: Fuck him!

(ROCCO *puts down the box, moves toward the record player.*)

(MICHAEL *goes to the box, takes a bottle out as...*)

MICHAEL: Have a drink with me. She wouldn't want us ta bury ourselves, would she?

(MICHAEL *drinks...as* ROCCO *removes the needle from the record.*)

MICHAEL: We gotta live, Rock, right? Live, Rocky, live.

(MICHAEL *puts the needle on the record, turns up the volume.* ROCCO *moves for the stereo—*MICHAEL *blocks him.*)

MICHAEL: Fuck him! Drink with me. C'mon! Have a drink.

(MICHAEL *turns the music even louder—blasting—and dances and drinks. He yells to be heard.*)

MICHAEL: Dance with me, Rocco! Have a drink, Rock! Dance! Dance with me! Snap with me, Rocco! Snap your fingers, Rocky! Snap. Snap. Snap.

(ROCCO *moves for the stereo,* MICHAEL *blocks his path.*)

MICHAEL: Snap. Snap. Snap.

ROCCO: Stop it.

MICHAEL: Snap. Snap. Snap.

ROCCO: Knock it off.

MICHAEL: Snap-snap-snap—

ROCCO: —Stop—

MICHAEL: —snap, snap, snap—

ROCCO: —stop—

MICHAEL: —snap, snap—

ROCCO: —HE'S SLEEPIN'!—

MICHAEL: —Fuck him!— *(Continues to drink/dance)*
—Snap. Snap. Snap. Snap. Snap. Snap. Snap... Drink
Rocky, snap-snap, move Rock, snap, snap, dance with
me, Rocky, live Rock, c'mon live, snap-snap-snap—

*(ROCCO grabs a bottle, but doesn't drink. MICHAEL
continues to dance and drink.)*

MICHAEL: —That's it, drink! Drink, Rocky, drink!

(ROCCO doesn't drink.)

MICHAEL: Snap. Move, Rocky, move. Feel it, c'mon
Rocky, dance, Rock... Snap-snap-snap—drink, drink,
drink—

(ROCCO takes his first drink in years.)

MICHAEL: —That's it, yes, yes, Rocky - Snap-snap-snap.
Move, Rock. Snap. Move. Snap.

(ROCCO snaps his fingers.)

MICHAEL: That's it, c'mon, snap. Snap, Rocky, snap-
snap-snap.

(ROCCO snaps and drinks.)

MICHAEL: Good, that's good, good! Move your feet,
Rocky! Move your feet. Dance. Move. Loosen up
man—live Rocky, live!

(ROCCO drinks.)

MICHAEL: YES! Move your feet, Rock. Move your feet!

(ROCCO moves his feet.)

MICHAEL: That's it. Shut your eyes. Close your eyes,
Rocky.

(ROCCO closes his eyes.)

MICHAEL: Snap. Snap. Move your feet. Stay your eyes
closed. Stay 'em closed, Rock. That's it. That's it.

*(ROCCO snaps his fingers, drinks, moves to the music, keeps
his eyes closed.)*

MICHAEL: Feel it, Rock. Feel. Feel, Rocky! Yes. Yes. Stay your eyes closed. Feel it. Feel it. Snap. Snap. Snap. Snap...

(ROCCO *slowly releases everything he has bottled-up. Everything he has "built". His movements grow in energy and ferocity. He moves quickly, freely. Almost wild. He is in his own world. Alone. Free)*

(MICHAEL *watches, staggers, smiles, celebrates.*)

MICHAEL: That's it, Rocky, that's it! Stay 'em closed, Rock. Yes! That's it! Stay 'em closed.

(MICHAEL *reaches for the duffel bag.*)

(ROCCO *dances. The music blasts.*)

(MICHAEL *watches* ROCCO *dancing across the room.*)

MICHAEL: Stay 'em closed, Rocky. That's it! You got it, Rock! You got it! That's it! Good! That's it! That's it! Just like that. (*He pulls a gun out of the duffel bag. He suddenly puts the barrel in his mouth and pulls the trigger—BANG!*)

(ROCCO *stops dancing. The music continues to blast.*)

(ROCCO *runs to his brother, grabs him in his arms, shakes him, tries to stop the blood from pouring out of the back of his head, all the while:*)

ROCCO: No— No—Mikey—Mikey— No— No—DAD! —DAD! —DAAAAD! —MIKEY! —NO! —NO! — MIKEY! —NO!

(*The music continues. He runs to the bottom of the stairs:*)

ROCCO: DAD!!!! DAAAADDDD!!!!!!

(ROCCO *runs to his brother, tries more pressure on the back of his head.*)

(*He runs to a phone. He dials.*)

ROCCO: (*Into phone*) 727 Ninth Street. 727 Ninth Street! 727 Ninth Street! 727! 727! (*He drops the phone, he runs*

to the bottom of the stairs:) DAD!! HURRY!! DAAAD!!
DAAAAAAAAAAD!!!!!!

(ROCCO runs to his brother. He takes him in his arms. He holds the back of his head. He rocks him back and forth.)

(The music continues to blast.)

ROCCO: No, no, no, no Mikey, no. I'm right here, Mikey. I'm right here, I'm right here...

(CHARLIE appears on the stairs. He stops halfway. He watches ROCCO cry and rock his brother in his arms.)

(ROCCO, still holding MICHAEL, looks up at CHARLIE.)

(CHARLIE turns and slowly exits up the stairs.)

(ROCCO continues to rock MICHAEL in his arms.)

(The song ends. The needle goes round and round on the record. ROCCO continues cradling MICHAEL in his arms.)

END OF ACT ONE

ACT TWO

(The same house. 9th Street. South Philadelphia)

(CHARLIE is in his easy chair. In his long-johns. A couple of cigars on the table next to him. And his swimmer's goggles. And a half-full scotch)

(ISABELLA, Puerto Rican, is on the couch, wearing a black dress, successfully suppressing a deep anger.)

(On the floor is her son, CARLITO, seven years old, sitting too close to the T V. The Sixers are playing the Bucks. He wears a black suit, tie and shoes. White socks)

(Other than the commentator on the T V... Silence)

(ROCCO enters from the kitchen. He wears his black suit pants, no tie, an unbuttoned white shirt with a tank-top underneath. He carries an Orange Crush with a straw, a glass of ice water and a scotch.)

(He gives the water to ISABELLA.)

ROCCO: Here ya go.

ISABELLA: Thanks.

(He gives CARLITO the Orange Crush.)

ROCCO: Orange Crush. My favorite.

CARLITO: Thank you.

(He keeps the scotch for himself. He holds it out for a toast. CARLITO clinks his bottle against the glass.)

ROCCO: Salud.

CARLITO: Salud.

(CARLITO *watches T V and drinks from his straw.* ROCCO *sits next to* CARLITO.)

CARLITO: *(Re: the game on T V)* Damn! *(To* ISABELLA*)* You see that? It's a wide-open layup!

ISABELLA: Turn it off.

CARLITO: *(To* ROCCO*)* Did you see that? He was wide-open.

ROCCO: Wide open.

(ISABELLA *gets up and turns off the T V. As she heads back for the couch...)*

CARLITO: It's the fourth quarter.

(ISABELLA *ignores* CARLITO. *She sits on the couch.)*

CARLITO: It's the fourth quarter.

(ISABELLA *ignores* CARLITO.*)*

(CHARLIE *puts on his swimmer's goggles. He lights a cigar.* CARLITO *looks at* CHARLIE. CHARLIE *ignores him. Then—)*

CARLITO: *(To* ISABELLA*)* What if I watch with the sound off?

(ISABELLA *looks at* CARLITO.*)*

CARLITO: Just for a little while?

(ISABELLA *gives an almost imperceptible nod of approval.)*

(CARLITO *moves to the T V, turns it on, and the sound down to silence.)*

(Pause)

ROCCO: Mo Cheeks is my favorite.

CARLITO: I like Doctor J.

ROCCO: Yeah. I like Doctor J too.

CARLITO: Me too. *(Looks at T V, pause, then:)* You like Moses?

ROCCO: Yeah.

CARLITO: Me too. *(Looks at T V, pause, then:)* You like Charles Barkley?

ROCCO: Yeah, "The Round Mound".

CARLITO: Me too. *(Looks at T V, pause, then:)* What about Andrew Toney?

ROCCO: I like him a lot. He can shoot.

CARLITO: Yeah?

ROCCO: Yeah.

CARLITO: Me too. *(He looks at the T V.)*

(Pause)

CHARLIE: I like Bobby Jones. The white guy.

CARLITO: I like Bobby Jones too. That means we both like him. Bobby Jones. That's cool.

(CHARLIE looks away. CARLITO continues looking at CHARLIE—fascinated by this man, his longjohns, his goggles. But also looking for some kind of approval—not getting any.)

(CARLITO once again looks to the T V.)

(Beat)

CHARLIE: *(To ISABELLA)* You're not wearing make-up.

ISABELLA: No.

CARLITO: Sometimes she wears red lipstick.

CHARLIE: I bet—an' a little red dress to go with it.

ROCCO: *(Changing the subject)* You know who your father useta really like was Freddie Brown. You know Freddie Brown? He played for the Sonics.

(CARLITO shakes his head "no".)

ROCCO: In Seattle. That's in Washington. In the *state* of Washington, all the way on the other side of America.

Above California. We useta...your father an' me... we
useta pretend we was on a plane flyin' there ta watch
him play. Freddie Brown. They called him Downtown
Freddie Brown. Cuz he could shoot from real far. From
Downtown.

CARLITO: Downtown Freddie Brown.

ROCCO: Yep. He once scored six thousand points in a
game.

CARLITO: Six thousand?

ROCCO: Yep.

CARLITO: Nuh-uh.

ROCCO: Did to.

CARLITO: No way.

ROCCO: He was your father's favorite. I bet you woulda
liked him.

CARLITO: I bet I woulda liked him too. Me an' my dad
always liked the same things. The same kindsa food,
the same players— *(To* ISABELLA*)* —What else we like
the same? Mom? Me an' Dad other'n food and players,
what else we like the same?

ISABELLA: Music.

CARLITO: *(To* ROCCO*)* Yeah, we both liked the same
music.

ROCCO: We'd pretend we was in the cockpit of the
plane, where the pilot sits. Your dad would be the
pilot, I'd be the co-pilot right aside him. We'd put
our hands like this. *(Mimes holding steering wheel)*
And pretend we had headphones on. And then
we'd fly. All the way the state a' Washington ta go
watch Downtown Freddie Brown. And we'd listen
ta music an' talk an' laugh. About how nice the state
a' Washington would be. 'Bout how happy Freddie

Brown would be ta see us. We'd keep our hands like this and fly away.

CARLITO: *(Mimes holding steering wheel)* Like this?

ROCCO: Yeah, an' like ya got headphones over your ears too, lissenin' ta control headquarters.

CARLITO: Hello control headquarters - this is Carlito, can you hear me?

ROCCO: I can hear ya loud an' clear, over n' out.

CARLITO: We're flying high in the sky, control headquarters.

ROCCO: An' ya look good doin' it. This is Rocco Molino, who'm I talkin' to, over n' out.

CARLITO: This is Carlito Molino, over n' out.

ROCCO: Ten-four, good buddy. Can you see the state a' Washington below your plane?

CARLITO: I think so. Can I?

ROCCO: You gotta look, like this.

(ROCCO looks, CARLITO looks.)

ROCCO: Ya see it?

CARLITO: I see it, good buddy.

ROCCO: Does it look as beautiful ta you as it does ta me?

CHARLIE: Oh, for chrissake, will ya?!

(Pause)

(ROCCO finishes his drink, stands.)

ROCCO: You want some more water, Izzie?

ISABELLA: No thanks.

ROCCO: How bout you, co-pilot? Ya want another Orange Crush?

CARLITO: Yes, please.

ISABELLA: One's enough.

CARLITO: But I want another one.

ISABELLA: You can have water. Do you want water?

CARLITO: No.

ISABELLA: *(To* ROCCO*)* Bring him a water.

*(*ROCCO *exits into the kitchen.)*

*(*CARLITO *defiantly slurps the remaining drops of Orange Crush through the straw.)*

CHARLIE: What kind of a name is Izzie? Sounds like a candy bar.

CARLITO: That's funny.

CHARLIE: Or a woman's drink—a Fizzy-Izzie.

CARLITO: That's funny too.

*(*Rocco *enters with a scotch for himself and a glass of water for* CARLITO.*)*

ISABELLA: *(To* CHARLIE*)* You don't like my name?

CHARLIE: It's just you people come up with a lotta names.

ISABELLA: It's Italian for Isabella.

CHARLIE: You ain't Italian.

ISABELLA: My mother liked Italian men.

CHARLIE: Your father's Italian?.

ISABELLA: No.

CHARLIE: I didn't think so.

CARLITO: *My* father's Italian.

CHARLIE: Your father's dead.

ROCCO: *(To* CHARLIE*)* So is yours.

ISABELLA: So is mine, so what?

(Beat)

CARLITO: I gotta pee.

ROCCO: It's through there, the other side the kitchen.

CARLITO: Is that where my daddy useta pee?

ROCCO: What?

CARLITO: When he lived here, is that where he peed?

ROCCO: Sometimes.

CARLITO: Is that where he peed when he was old as me? Is that where his bedroom was?

ROCCO: You wanna see his bedroom?

CARLITO: Yes, please.

ROCCO: It's got a toilet up there your daddy useta pee in all the time. You can pee in it too if ya want.

CARLITO: Is his bed still there?

ROCCO: It's got everything. Just the way he left it.

CARLITO: *(To* ISABELLA*)* Could I go?

ISABELLA: Go on.

CARLITO: *(To* ROCCO*)* Come on co-pilot, let's go.

ROCCO: Ten-four, good buddy.

CARLITO: Ten-four.

*(*CARLITO *and* ROCCO *exit up the stairs.)*

(Long pause)

ISABELLA: He shoulda shot you instead. If he even shot himself in the first place. It's why he brought his gun. He didn't leave a note. It's why he wanted to come alone. I wanted him to come sooner, with Carlito. Before your wife...I wanted our son to meet his family. He said no. He said he needed to respect his mother's wishes ta never come back. He said you'd kill'm if he ever did. I wish he shot you instead. If I had a gun I'd do it myself.

CHARLIE: You want me ta get one for you?

ISABELLA: I want you ta shut the fuck up. *(At some point she rises, moves toward* CHARLIE.*)* He did what he did to that drunk driver for *you.* He named our son after you. He's my son too. He is your grand child. He carries your name—Carlito, Little Charlie. Say something nice to him. Tell him you like his new suit. Tell him you like his eyes. Tell him he reminds you of his father. Tell him you were too sad to attend his father's funeral, your own son's funeral. You were too sad and that's why you weren't there. He was your *son,* you couldn't go the three blocks? He was your *son.* And for whatever I can't figure out, he loved you. Say something nice to his son. You will never get a second chance. You will tell my boy something nice about *himself*—and something nice about his father. And then we'll leave you alone. You'll never see him again. You'll never get a chance to *hurt* him. And if you *do*—if you hurt him—with your hateful, bitter, racist, die-alone-in-that-fucking-chair shit—on the day he buried his dad—I will hurt *you.* I will return, I will hunt you down, and I will *kill* you. I don't give a shit if you're friends with Nicky Scarfo or Vito-fuckin'-Corleone, if you hurt my child...I will take a *knife*...and I will cut your throat. I will cut out your fucking throat.

*(*CHARLIE *remains still, calm. He takes a sip of his drink.)*

*(*ISABELLA *walks to the wall with the photo of Joanie. She stares.)*

ISABELLA: Your wife, your daughter and your son.

(While running down the stairs:)

CARLITO: Mom, mom, mommy!!! *(He enters, carrying a poster.)* Look, it's Downtown Freddie Brown, Uncle Rocco gave it to me, he was Daddy's favorite player—he's givin' me daddy's old clothes too—hurry up!! *(He runs back up the stairs.)*

ISABELLA: *(To* CHARLIE*)* An hour ago he buried his father.

*(*ISABELLA *exits up the stairs.* CHARLIE *remains. He smokes. He drinks. He doesn't move.)*

CHARLIE: Rocco! *(Beat)* Rocky! *(Pause)* ROCCO!

(Pause)

*(*CHARLIE *stands, goes to the stereo. He puts on Vic Damone's* An Affair to Remember*. He remains on his feet as he listens. He closes his eyes.)*

*(*ROCCO *comes down the stairs [After lyric "time and space"]) He goes to the stereo and aggressively removes the needle from the record, making a loud scratching sound.)*

*(*CHARLIE *suddenly slaps* ROCCO *hard across the face.)*

(Running down the stairs, we hear:)

CARLITO: Uncle Rocco, Uncle Rocco! *(He reaches the bottom of the stairs. He's wearing a Phillies Little League jersey.)* Can I have this too? It says "Molino" on back, it fits perfect!

*(*ISABELLA *appears half-way down the stairs.* MICHAEL*'s childhood clothing is draped over her arms.)*

ROCCO: It wasn't your father's, it's mine.

CARLITO: It fits perfect.

ROCCO: You could have it if ya want.

CARLITO: Hell yeah!

*(*ISABELLA *smacks the back of* CARLITO*'s head.)*

CARLITO: *(To* ROCCO*)* I mean, yes, please.

ROCCO: It's all yours.

CARLITO: For reals?

ROCCO: It says "Molino" don't it? That's your name.

ISABELLA: Give your uncle a hug.

(CARLITO hugs ROCCO.)

CARLITO: Thank you.

(CARLITO turns and hugs CHARLIE, who doesn't hug him back.)

CARLITO: Thank you.

(CARLITO stops hugging CHARLIE and looks up at him. No response. He walks back toward ISABELLA as:)

CARLITO: *(To ROCCO)* She picked a lotta daddy's clothes, look. A lot of 'em don't even fit, I'm already so big.

(While...CHARLIE sits in his chair. He puts on his goggles. He lights a cigar. And ROCCO puts the Vic Damone record back in its sleeve.)

(ISABELLA moves toward the front door.)

CARLITO: Where you going?

(Standing near the coat rack:)

ISABELLA: Say goodbye, we have a bus to catch.

CARLITO: But I don't wanna go yet.

ISABELLA: Say goodbye.

ROCCO: I'll see ya again lil fella. Okay?

(CARLITO just nods.)

ROCCO: We'll fly airplanes, wherever you wanna go that's where we'll go. Okay?

CARLITO: Okay. *(He walks over to CHARLIE, sitting in his chair. To CHARLIE)* Good bye.

(CHARLIE looks at CARLITO. Says nothing. Turns away)

(CARLITO and ISABELLA head for the exit.)

CHARLIE: C'mere. *(Beat)* Come over here.

(CARLITO *looks at* ISABELLA—*she gives no approval, but doesn't stop him either.* CHARLIE *snuffs out his cigar, takes off his goggles.*)

CHARLIE: Siddown.

(CARLITO *moves toward* CHARLIE.)

CHARLIE: Sit.

(CARLITO *sits in a nearby chair.*)

CHARLIE: Closer.

(CARLITO *moves the chair closer. He sits. He looks at* CHARLIE.)

(CHARLIE *looks at* CARLITO.)

(ISABELLA *and* ROCCO *watch.*)

(*Pause*)

CARLITO: Yes?

CHARLIE: Yes. You live in Pittsburgh. When your father was your age...he lived here. South Philadelphia.

CARLITO: I know.

CHARLIE: Let me finish. (*Pause*) I've been here my whole life. In this house. (*Beat*) Some things you gotta learn on your own. (*Beat*) More than a...over a hundred years ago...

CARLITO: ...What?—

CHARLIE: —Let me finish. Over a hundred years ago. Kensington, up the road. A mechanic, a father...he took his three children in a rowboat. On the river. A man... was doing a good thing for his children. Paddling a boat on a river. They fished. (*Beat*) After sundown, he needed to get them home, for supper, ta have their mother grill the fish. They paddled 'round the south end a' Petty's Island, not far. There was another boat. A tug boat, just doin' his job—no children, no fishing. Just doin' his job. It was getting dark. It didn't see the

rowboat. By the time it saw, it blew its whistle—but it
was too late. The father—he was the only one didn't
die. His three children—six, nine and fifteen. The father
swam out there all night, looking for his kids. Hopin'
he might find at least one who didn't drown. He didn't
find any. He had ta go home and tell his wife. *(Pause)*
There is nothing worse. *(Pause)* I was too sad to attend
your father's funeral. *(Beat)* I was too sad to go the
three blocks to the church. *(Beat)* Your *father*...Charlie.
(Beat) Carlito. (Beat) You're a...you're a handsome boy.
Someday I hope you become a man. Your father was a
man. He was not a little boy. *Once* he was a little boy...
but he grew into a man. He was a good man. He made
choices. Men make choices. They take action. They
are not little boys. Some little boys grow up to become
men. Other little boys remain little boys no matter
how old their birth certificate says. Even if it says
they're *older* than their younger brother. They believe
in magic and make-believe. They do nothing. They are
ungrateful. They live with their parents until they die.
Little boys their whole lives. *(Beat)* Grow up to be a
man. Like your father. You remind me of him when he
was your age.

(Pause)

(CHARLIE *puts the cigar in his mouth. He begins to put the
goggles over his eyes. He hesitates.)*

(He puts the goggles over CARLITO's *eyes. He then looks
away, straight ahead, remains still, silent.)*

(CARLITO *continues to stare at him.)*

ISABELLA: Let's go. *(Beat)* Carlito.

(CARLITO *looks over to* ISABELLA, *the swimmer's goggles
over his eyes.)*

ISABELLA: Let's go.

(CARLITO *walks to the front door, still wearing the goggles.)*

(ROCCO *walks over.* ISABELLA *opens the door,* CARLITO *exits.*)

ROCCO: I'm sorry.

ISABELLA: For what?

ROCCO: I dunno. I think a lotta things.

ISABELLA: *(Beat)* ...Thanks.

(ISABELLA *exits.* ROCCO *watches them go. He closes the door.*)

(*He stares at his father, who ignores him.*)

(*Pause*)

ROCCO: I know whatchyou was talkin' 'bout, Pop. *(Pause)* I know whatchyou was talkin' 'bout. *(Pause)* I know whatchyou was sayin'. *(Beat)* I KNOW WHATCHYOU WAS TALKIN' ABOUT!

(*No response from* CHARLIE.)

(ROCCO *walks to a bookshelf, opens a cabinet underneath. He pulls out the Ouija Board. He puts it on the dining room table. He puts his hands over the planchette. He shuts his eyes. His hands drift slowly around the board. He opens his eyes and watches his hands move around the board.*)

(*He looks at his dad, who still ignores him, staring straight ahead. He stands. He goes to the stereo. He puts the Stevie Ray Vaughn album on the turntable. He lowers the needle.*)

(Mary Had a Little Lamb [live] *begins to play.*)

(*He looks at his father—no response.*)

(*He turns it up a little louder.*)

(*He looks at his father—no response.*)

(*Then a little louder. No response*)

(ROCCO *begins to move a little, dance a little. He drinks. He dances, moving toward* CHARLIE. *He stops six-eight feet away. He looks at his father.*)

(CHARLIE doesn't respond, doesn't so much as glance in ROCCO's direction.)

(ROCCO continues to stare. Dance. Ready himself)

(ROCCO quickly takes a couple of steps with purpose—then suddenly stops, just a couple of feet away.)

(CHARLIE turns to face him:)

CHARLIE: Go on. *(Beat)* Do it, Rocky! *(Beat)* What're you waiting for? FUCKING DO IT!

(Quickly, ROCCO lunges and wraps his hands around CHARLIE's neck, choking him. CHARLIE doesn't fight it. He does his best to try to NOT fight it. To resist his natural, instinctual response to survive. He does his best to keep his hands on the arm rests of the easy chair.)

(The music continues.)

(ROCCO chokes and chokes and chokes...then suddenly stops.)

(ROCCO cries and collapses on CHARLIE's chest, hugging him, gently touching his neck as he apologizes.)

ROCCO: I'm sorry, I'm sorry...I'm sorry...I'm sorry, Pop...I'm sorry...I'm sorry...I'm sorry...

(The music continues.)

(ROCCO wipes his tears. CHARLIE rubs his neck.)

(ROCCO moves to the record player and lifts the needle.)

(Silence)

(ROCCO looks at CHARLIE.)

(Pause)

ROCCO: I'm sorry Pop. *(Pause)* I'm sorry.

(CHARLIE looks at ROCCO.)

ROCCO: I'm sorry.

(Long pause)

CHARLIE: I forgive you.

(Long pause)

ROCCO: You hungry? *(Beat)* Ya want somethin' ta eat?

(CHARLIE holds out his glass.)

(ROCCO walks over, takes the glass, heads for the kitchen. Before he enters the kitchen:)

CHARLIE: Rocky?

(ROCCO stops.)

CHARLIE: Play me my song. *(Beat)* Not too loud. *(Beat)* Be sure to turn down the volume.

(ROCCO removes Stevie Ray Vaughn, turns down the volume knob, then puts on Vic Damone's An Affair to Remember.*)*

(He enters the kitchen as the song plays.)

(CHARLIE stares straight ahead.)

(Long pause)

(ROCCO enters from the kitchen, a glass of scotch in each hand.)

(He puts one on the table next to his father—CHARLIE doesn't touch it.)

(ROCCO goes to the dining room table, sits. Drinks)

(He puts his hand over the Ouija's planchette. He allows the planchette to move his hands about the board.)

(CHARLIE remains, still, calm, listening to the music. Staring at the stereo.)

(The song ends.)

(Silence... Other than the needle going round and round on the turntable.)

(CHARLIE continues looking toward the stereo. Then stops... and stares straight ahead.)

(ROCCO *continues with the Ouija board.*)

(An eternity)

END OF PLAY

www.ingramcontent.com/pod-product-compliance
Lightning Source LLC
Chambersburg PA
CBHW070033110426
42741CB00035B/2755